SOUL FIRE
Cafe

Making Peace with the One in the Mirror

Lesia Zablockij

DISCLAIMER

This book is based, in part, upon actual events but is also a work of creative nonfiction. The stories are written strictly from the perspective, opinion and memory of the writer. Some names and identifying details have been changed to protect the privacy of the people involved.

DEDICATION

This book is dedicated to my husband,
Wasyl,
for having more faith in me
than I ever had in myself.

I dedicate this book to you
to honour the man that you are
and to thank you for the support
you have always given me as
you stood by my side through it all.

I love you always my umpty-umkin.

ACKNOWLEDGEMENTS

A book is never the effort of one person. I can truly say this book would not be published without the encouragement and support of my friends, John and Jana Baron.

Jana, you have been my sounding board for so many years. I so thank you for the two minute phone calls "to bounce something off of you" that turn into one hour phone calls. That's such a small part of how you have supported me over the years that thank you doesn't seem sufficient. How fortunate am I and others that cross your path!

John, I thank you for your proofreading, your constructive criticism, giving up time that you would rather spend with "Blush" and for keeping me laughing. You have been there in a snap if there was anything you could do to help.

John, Jana and Wasyl – thank you all for being my guinea pigs as I trained and tried out different tests on you. I hope we learned more about each other along the way.

Thank you Minette Riordan - "The Artful Marketer" and my coach for kicking me in the pants when I needed it. Thank you for all you do to keep me on track. Your gentle nudging played a big part in completing this book.

Most importantly, I humbly offer my sincere thanks to my clients who have allowed me in and shared their stories and their tears until they became smiles. You are all extremely brave souls and you have my deepest gratitude and respect. The people staring back at you in the mirror have rejuvenated their soul fire and I couldn't be more proud. May you keep the soul fires burning!

FOREWORD

Have you ever wondered what happiness is? The book you hold may help you understand more about this often asked question. The stories are sad and yet happy and a must read for anyone wanting more in life or simply want help in understanding themselves.

I have been a client for over 5 years and worked through 4 different programs for varying reasons such as happiness, change, goals, death and life in general. They were all stepping stones in my life's path and my growth as an individual.

This book could only be written by someone who has been there. I watched Lesia struggle through some of the hardest moments of her life and I witnessed her growth. I know she is equipped to help others because I lived it with her and I have seen the changes. She has a way of asking questions that help you dig deep but not feel threatened. The intent is never to harm but only to encourage healing and I have seen her do this over and over again.

Lesia is a unique person who sincerely cares and you won't be disappointed by reading this light but serious conversation between two strangers who become respectful friends and develop calm and happy hearts. If you don't know where to start, this book is a good first step.

With Gratitude,
Jana Lee Baron
February 2015

For only we can determine if we are to be just another painting or a masterpiece.

Jovan

Introduction

If anyone had told me that my life would have changed this much I would never have believed it. A family of 12 that spent most of their time together became only the two of us in a few short years. I was stunned and in disbelief that this had happened and yet I knew there had been signs along the way.

As I struggled to make my way through the upside down version of my new world, I began to search for meaning. What was I supposed to do? How would I cope? When would I stop hurting?

In that search I questioned many things that I once believed to be true in my life. Things I assumed and took for granted. Things I believed would remain constant for the most part.

I was no longer the caregiver, the daughter, the sister, the sister-in-law, the confidante or the aunt. All my roles seem to disappear, evaporating into thin air. Without those things, I had to figure out the answer to the question "Who am I now?" What a huge question that turned out to be.

It took a long time. It took strength I didn't believe I would ever find. I went through so many emotions as I tried to make sense of all the changes, the emptiness, the sadness and the pain. I think the total disregard and the way people can cut you out of their lives with no look back was the most confusing. I had no idea who these people were anymore and perhaps I never really did.

I thought we were close. I was wrong.

I thought we would always have each other's back. I was wrong.

I thought we had a bond that was unbreakable. I was wrong.

And most of all, I thought we meant something to each other and I was so wrong.

First, there was a death, then a divorce, then illness, then a second death, then a second divorce. The family was torn apart and there was no way to heal it. In the middle of all of it, friendships were lost and most other relationships fell apart as well.

For me, the healing seemed to take forever. As time went on I became aware that if things hadn't changed, I would still be doing what I was doing with the same people. I would not have moved on to do what I should be doing and discover things about myself, people and life.

I would never have written this book. I would not have been blessed to meet some of the people with whom I have since crossed paths. I would not have found the tools to help others in pain. I would have been content to live in oblivion as so many of the ones I left behind.

To help my shattered heart, I read, I wrote, I trained and became certified in modalities that had served to help my growth and eventually the growth of others. I questioned things that I took for granted like the meaning of family, honesty, integrity, loyalty, trust and even my religious upbringing. All of the things that made me who I was. Most importantly, I looked at what those things meant to me and what they may have meant to others I once spent all my time with. I realized how little we actually had in common outside the "family". Our values were so different. How could I have been so blind?

What I discovered and what I now truly believe is that we all have lessons to learn in our lifetime. I have noticed that if a lesson is not learned the first time around, those lessons continue to show themselves in different ways affording us the opportunity to try once more to see the lesson. I have asked and have seen others ask questions like "What am I not getting?" or "What don't I see here?" or the biggie "Why does this keep happening to me?" Those questions come up more often than you might think. I sometimes questioned myself and watched others question themselves as well.

I set out seeking the answers to those questions. I studied various personality assessments. I studied grief and grief recovery. I studied life coaching. I studied storytelling and the beliefs we live behind that may not be our own. I tried to understand what happened from a logical viewpoint but you can't make logical sense out of illogical events.

Eventually, others came along looking for answers to their questions. Still others were sent to me. The common thread was that these people were in transition. They were stuck because at this point in their life, something had changed and they could no longer make sense of their own lives. They didn't know what the next step was. They didn't know what they were supposed to do and they didn't know what their role was in their new life.

Having been forced to figure that out for myself, I was able to coach many through hard times to a place of peace. I also found, you never connect with another person without learning more about yourself.

I became aware (mostly by people pointing it out to me), that many come to me because I provided a safe place for them to open their hearts without fear or judgment and to explore what's within them. They find the source of pain in their heart and then discover the reason or reasons for it. Surprisingly, what happens is people find that the cause of their pain was often not what they thought it was. So how do you heal something that you are unaware of? Surprisingly, because of what I had gone through, I was able to help. I had started to find my way home.

I have listened to some painful stories from truly brave individuals. I was amazed that some remained standing after the things they had experienced. I listened and was honoured to be allowed to hear their stories and hopefully helped them release their pain. I was with them while they did the work to get through the dark tunnel to the other side. It was hard at times but I have not heard anyone say it wasn't worth it.

Through coaching clients and being coached and mentored myself, I have come to realize that being able to provide a safe place for others is a gift. It was a gift I was unaware of and being unaware, I certainly had not appreciated or embraced it.

As I worked with clients, I saw a theme arise about broken relationships, whether they were family, friendships, co-workers or partners. It was heartbreaking but I could easily relate to their feelings. We trust and love unconditionally but that sometimes is not enough or sadly, doesn't matter in the end.

I do not like to see people in pain and suffering. I often feel compelled to step in, sometimes at my own peril. I look around and see unfairness and injustice. There is little reason for many situations to turn out the way they do.

Years ago I remember my mother in her later years not watching the news as it was too heartbreaking for her to see the suffering in the world. I understand that now and since she was always such a blessing in my life, perhaps that is a part of her I carry with me. She didn't like the pain humanity causes one another and it showed in her kindness and love for us. She was always my angel and probably still is.

Global catastrophes happen and are horrific and disturbing but it's what I observe or hear about close to home in the casual everyday ways that people hurt each other that is even more upsetting. When did it become that the only way to move forward in life is to become adversarial or narcissistic? What happened to being accountable for your part in a situation and both sides trying to find a way to improve it and heal?

What I have seen is that often one side does not want to be wrong and there is no path of reconciliation when that happens. Why can't they both admit to being partly wrong and move past it? Instead they harbour hatred, resentment and anger and that's no way to live your life. The estrangement in families and relationships that has happened because someone has to be right is senseless but I have seen it more and more. Is it really so important to be right?

I have also seen the effects of loss on people's lives. When people hear the word "loss" or "grief", it is so limiting. Most people automatically relate it to death but there are so many more losses that have the same effect on a person and require grieving and closure. Some of those losses can be divorce, job loss, moving, retirement, financial change and loss of health to the point of a terminal illness to name a few.

Other events that people don't relate to grief but carry the same effects are loss of trust, loss of faith and loss of self. It is the loss of self that I am focusing on here because the loss of self can occur as a result of many other losses.

I believe loss is "Any event that changes your life from that moment forward". Whether it's good or bad, it may need to be addressed so it doesn't cause difficulties in your future.

For example, you make a decision to take a better job. You love your current job and the people you work with but you make this choice to advance yourself. Great decision for you but still a loss and you may feel sadness. You may miss who you were in that old job and what you are leaving behind. That loss can cause grief even if it really is a happy decision.

I have written this book with its stories to help you find the fire in your soul just as I had to. I encourage you to move beyond the dark days, manoeuver the bumps in the road and cut the invisible chains that hold you to a past that no longer serves you. Past events can create beliefs that may not be true and unless those beliefs are unearthed, challenged and discredited, they remain intact and may even paralyze you.

I hope you will once again discover who you truly are and stop believing someone else's opinion of who they think you are or should be.

It is my belief that if you are not happy or satisfied with parts of your life, it is very possible it is because *someone said or didn't say*, or *someone did or didn't do* something that made you change your opinion of yourself. Whether it was deliberate or not, the effect is often carried throughout your life and can only be changed if you recognize it, address it and then heal it. It all begins with awareness. Sometimes an individual may not know how to access that awareness without a helping hand and those helping hands are out there.

The human spirit seems to be failing. Many have given up, become complacent and stopped caring or believing in themselves. They have settled for "**what is**" instead of believing in and striving for "**what is possible**". Moving one foot in front of the other is how they go through life.

They have let their dreams die or perhaps were never able to connect to those dreams in the first place. That's the tragedy of the soul and I believe it doesn't have to be that way. This is our life and we should be living it while we can. Make a choice to grow through life instead.

So, I ask you to take a step forward. See if a version of yourself appears in any of the stories that follow. The stories that moved me to a place where

I had to do things differently. Hopefully they provide a glimmer of hope and a way to reconnect with a deeper and happier you. Perhaps these stories will provide a way to believe once again in who you truly are and help you find your way back to you. And for now, if the strength just isn't there, remember, you can hold on to my strength. The strength that I had to find to rebuild from my losses. The strength that exists now because of the ones that left my life. You are never alone. Help is always within reach. Sometimes you have to just trust a little and open your heart to see it.

    I invite you to take a journey with Myla and Jane; two people who formed a friendship over coffee. Through conversation and coffee, they rekindle the fire in their souls. They find hope as they examine family, relationships, the future and life itself.

    It's about making peace with the one in the mirror. May they help you do the same!

A man/woman is not old until regrets take the place of dreams.

John Barrymore

WHEN LIFE CHANGES

Jane's head was spinning as she sat staring at the blank paper in front of her. She could imagine her straight dark hair was standing on end as she kept running her hands through it in frustration. It was a bad habit borne out of anxiety. She just couldn't think clearly enough to even try to make sense of what her life had become. Someone suggested that writing might be helpful but so far the paper was not very welcoming. She didn't even know where to start. Feeling like an empty shell, she had no idea who she was anymore. All that was important to her no longer existed.

Jane had been coming to Soul Fire Cafe for some time now. It wasn't a very busy place but her favourite waitress always had fresh coffee brewing. Today Jane was here hoping to find some peace of mind.

Jane had been devoted to her family and spent a lot of time with them but that family no longer formed a part of her life. The reality of it all was still hard for her to grasp. She couldn't understand how this could happen.

She looked around the small coffee shop trying to find something although she wasn't really sure what she was looking for. Perhaps some answers would drop out of the air for her but it didn't seem like that would happen. With heaviness in her heart, she looked back at the blank paper and started feeling the tears welling up in her eyes yet again. The stillness was broken with a "How you doin' hon?"

She was jolted back to reality as she looked up to see the familiar face smiling from ear to ear. Myla was always cheerful. Her blond curly hair and that red lipstick outlining that radiant smile may have been just what she was looking for that day.

"What can I get ya Jane?"

"Coffee. Black please Myla."

"You got it!" Myla spun around and seemed to return with the coffee in seconds, still smiling. She moved so quickly even though she had an extra pound or two. She seemed to glide through the café.

"Thanks Myla."

Jane sipped the coffee and watched this woman bounce around the shop. She looked like she had the world by the tail. But wait, life will throw her a curve ball and wipe that smile off her face one day.

Ouch!! She didn't really want that to happen to Myla at all. It was just a reflection of Jane's state of mind. It was definitely time to work out some of that bitterness.

She continued to stare at the paper that she hoped would be her salvation. It just stared right back at her.

Myla popped by with the coffee pot." If you don't mind me sayin', you seem a tad disheartened today."

Jane sighed, "Yeah I suppose I am Myla; just life and trying to sort it out. Don't want to burden you with my sad story. Still trying to make sense of it myself and not having a lot of luck."

"Good luck with that Jane. I don't mean to pry but it looks like you could use a friend."

Jane laughed, "You might be right. This blank paper doesn't seem to be cooperating."

Myla smiled. "I can tell ya - life is life and there ain't no way to sort it out. The hardest thing in the world is trying to figure out why people do the things they do. And if you ever figure it out (or think you have), they turn around and do something completely different and you are back at square one. We are an interesting bunch, us humans!"

Jane nodded. "I'll say! I can't believe that things that have happened with the people I once shared my life with. Most have become complete strangers."

"Aaah! Must be family!"

Jane nodded and felt her jaw clench.

"Jane, they're the hardest to figure out! We think cause they're family they will do no harm. If and when they do, we are caught by such surprise. We think they know us, love us and will do so forever. Not so, is it?" Now, don't get me wrong. I'm not saying family is bad but they are still *people* just like anybody else.

I guess we hold them up to a higher bar because they are *"family"* and that is what society has drilled into us so we believe it. However, all the players are different with their own ideas and values and sometimes that doesn't make for a long-lasting relationship, family or not.

Every person deals with life as a result of what they have witnessed or what has happened to them. It doesn't matter if they are family or not, you cannot be with them every moment of the day and see what happens in their life. Everybody is unique just like every relationship. You can have two people in a relationship with the same person and each relationship is completely different because their viewpoint is different."

"I hear you Myla, I just don't understand why someone turns on you for apparently no reason. They disrupt the family just to make it easier to walk away. Why not just be honourable and do what you need to do without blaming or hurting others to make yourself feel better."

"You see Jane, you are looking at this through your eyes. You would do the honourable thing because that is what you've been taught and that is who you have become. You weren't raised in the same way as someone else was raised. You didn't experience what they did. As a result, your value system is different."

"Yes that is very true. You know, it's interesting Myla. Even my father saw this person for what she was from day one. If only we had all been that wise! Perhaps what's harder to get over is that I saw what she was too. I never trusted her and knew she would cause damage but yet I allowed her into my life and even welcomed her."

Why Jane? Why did you do that? Do you know the answer?

"Sadly Myla, I do. She became part of the family. She entered what I believed to be the inner sanctum of "the family". This warranted her protection and inclusion. I can't believe how naïve I was!"

"Jane, you were acting out of a place of trust and acceptance and that's understandable. When you looked at her family, was the dynamic of their inner circle the same as yours?"

Jane tossed her head back, "Hah! Absolutely not! I knew my family had my back. The dysfunction in her family was huge. Never have I seen such different siblings and there was no connection between any of them. They were different in looks, in attitudes and lifestyles. There was no common thread between them at all."

"So you recognize that now Jane. Why not then?"

"Oh Myla, I didn't in the beginning. She was coming into our family and I didn't look at or really even see hers for that matter. But, after some time, I saw how easily discarded her family or friends were but by then it was too late. Why I would think it would be any different with ours, I'll never know. I did see it at other times but again I chose to overlook it for the sake of the inner circle. Not trusting my own intuition cost me and others in the end.

Myla nodded. "I do believe that people generally show us who they are. It is hard to hide your true nature for any length of time. It is we who choose not to see the truth. I'm not saying to be paranoid or run away from relationships. What I mean is if your instincts are giving you clues, pay attention to them. Our intuition is there to help us and it looks like you chose to overlook what it was telling you."

"I so did Myla and I did it in a big way! I did it for the right reasons and for the wrong reasons. I chose to ignore the signs to keep peace in the family. I did it to not buck choices family members made and respect their decisions. There was no way I could stop the insanity once this individual showed her true colours."

"Well Jane we will have to talk more but I should get back to my other customers. You have a good day."

"Thanks Myla. It's a little better since talking to you."

And with that she smiled and bounced over to her next customer.

Jane sat for a moment and watched Myla. She had come hoping to do some writing but instead chatted with Myla and found some new things to think about. With that, she left the coffee shop feeling a little lighter.

A Moment for You:

Pay attention to your gut instinct. If your intuition is making your tummy twinge or the hair on the back of your neck stand up, pay attention. Our instincts exist to guide us and keep us safe. Give it some thought and protect yourself.

Is there something or someone in your world that causes a physical or emotional reaction in you by their actions or words? Why do you think you are having this reaction? What can you do to keep yourself safe or protected?

Real power is measured by how much you can let things go.

D.H. Thoreau

THE FLY IN THE OINTMENT

Jane was sitting at the table enjoying her hot cup of coffee when Myla popped out from behind the swinging doors.

"Good day Myla. Nice to see you."

"Hi there Jane."

"Myla you sure made me think last time we spoke. It made me think about things in a whole new way. I do want to thank you again for that." Jane chuckled and said, "Can I buy you a coffee?"

Myla spun around and seeing they were alone in the shop, she plunked herself down and poured herself a coffee. They both laughed.

Jane began, "You know, I was thinking about some of the damage caused by the person I spoke of last time. She not only separated herself from the family but tore the children away. These children were around these family members from the day they were born and were part of the reason they loved to spend time together."

Jane paused and then continued, "I always felt her actions were based on her strange perception of disloyalty. If she felt a person didn't side with her, they would be tossed aside. What type of person does that to friends and family? What type of mother does that to her children? The children were young. You have heard the term "It takes a village to raise a child"?"

Myla nodded.

"Unfortunately Myla, she removed the village and she was ill-equipped to raise them on her own."

"Ah yes Jane, but remember you are looking at things the way you would like to do them. Your expectation is that she would do things the right way and that was obviously not the way she operated. Her main focus was herself and it sounds like she would rather be alone than feel threatened by anyone's disloyalty. Sad really! Wonder where that kind of threat started?"

Jane nodded. "You know, I think you are right. I have seen her turn people away at the drop of a hat and over the years she has done the same to her children. I guess I'm thankful I don't think that way and I am thankful this person is no longer in my life. Such ridiculous drama because of unwarranted insecurity!"

"I can tell you of a similar situation" Myla added. "A friend of mine stood by a family member and was beaming with joy for her sibling's child as she achieved a prestigious award, she said to her sibling "You must be so proud". She was so stunned when the response was "Well, you should have had your own children and then you would know."

"Jane, this friend was not only acknowledging her sibling's child's success but her success as a parent. It was like being slapped in the face. But you know it's like I say, people react to things because of their life and the experiences they have had in their own lives. You never really know how unhappy someone is unless they tell you."

"My friend knew she couldn't change what was said. She certainly couldn't understand it either. The only possible thing she could change was her reaction to it. Slowly she realized it was not about her but rather about some strange idea this person had even though it certainly felt like it was about her at the time." Right or wrong, it happened. She could have chosen to beat her head against a brick wall trying to change or understand it but that would have been painful not to mention futile. For her to move on, she had to choose to let it go.

"From past reference, there was no talking to this person. The defences were always up and she always seemed to be in attack mode. My friend didn't know why she spoke to her that way but she decided she didn't need to know. She just had to keep herself from harm's way and that is exactly what she did. Again, truly sad!"

"You see Jane, people waste so much energy being angry and defensive to the point where I don't think they even remember what they are angry or defensive about. It becomes a way of life for them. I can't imagine how exhausting it must be to carry that kind of anger with you all the time. That's not the way I choose to live, at least not anymore" and she smiled.

"Now Jane, I'm not saying that things don't catch me off guard. They do. But, I try to breathe and take a step back before I react. It doesn't always work but when it does, it really helps minimize the drama in my life. Sometimes it works, sometimes not so much, but I keep trying. It's a lifelong thing I think."

"I hear you Myla and it makes a lot of sense. How do you manage to not react? I mean, let's face it, sometimes situations can be pretty upsetting and it's hard to keep calm."

"Yes Jane. So true. I have been there. All I can say is it takes practice. Stopping for a moment after an over-reaction by someone else gives me the chance to say "WOW – where's that coming from? Can this really be about me?" I wonder what's going on in their world. Rather than escalate things which I once would have done, I try to not be so defensive and see what happens. It keeps peace in my world that way."

"Sounds tough old girl."

"It can be Jane. With practice it gets easier but it takes continual stepping back and reassessing. Think about this. If you can think of a situation where someone over-reacted and then think about what you did to get such a reaction. Think about it. Did what you did really warrant that type of reaction? Often it doesn't. It's often a case of being in the wrong place at the right time and being in the line of fire. Unfortunately, some bullets just can't be dodged."

"Like the situation I just described, my friend gave a huge compliment and was pretty much slapped on the face. It was a completely strange and over-the-top reaction. She did nothing wrong and certainly meant no malice. It was a statement of pure joy and pride. The reaction made absolutely no sense so she stepped back to get out of the line of any continued fire."

'The unfortunate thing is people that always see the worse and are always on the defensive, never see it as an over-reaction. They feel completely justified with their reaction and they are never wrong. You can never make sense of that kind of logic.'

'I have to add, taking responsibility for your part is also important if you want to live in integrity. We all have our part in most situations and owning up is important, especially owning up to ourselves. After all, if you can't see yourself for who you truly are, how can you make any changes if changes are necessary?'

'Jane, I can certainly see that accountability is something you value. So being careful not to play the blame game is important. Being honest with yourself can be quite humbling at times but there's often a lesson to be learned within that honesty.'

Just then the bell above the door rang. Myla stood up. "Duty Calls."

"Thanks Myla. You have a great day." I watched her get a fresh pot of coffee to bring to her new guests. As I watched her, I mused at how this woman had a PhD from the U of Common Sense and I was learning so much from her. Perhaps they were things I already knew but somehow it was different from Myla. She had a way that opened my eyes and mind just a little wider. I knew I needed to do that to stop hurting and it was helping thanks to Myla.

A Moment for You

People do things for their own reasons. You may never understand or even know those reasons.

It's a waste of energy trying to figure out what someone could possibly be thinking. If you have spent some time trying to come up with an answer and you can't, it probably won't happen. Quit wasting your time, your emotions and depleting your energy trying to come up with an answer that is plausible to you. You will probably not come up with an answer that brings you any satisfaction and no certainty that you are correct as you will never know.

As hurtful as any comment someone makes towards you, their reason for doing so will probably never reveal itself. Even if you asked them, you may never know the truth. They may not even know themselves.

Is there something you need to let go of for your own peace? Give it some thought and make peace with it for your sake. They have not given it a second thought so why waste your time trying to figure it out.

Try viewing everyone who comes into your life as a teacher.

Wayne Dyer

THE LOSS THAT CRACKED THE SEAL

"Myla, have you ever had the good fortune to know an individual that makes everyone want to be a better person because of that person? My mother was such a person. She was kind, understanding and always, loved her family unconditionally. Her family was like air to her; all she needed was them and they all knew it, felt it and bloomed because of it. This trust and acceptance made all of us never want to disappoint her."

"Sounds like you were very lucky to have had her in your life Jane."

"Yes, we were all blessed Myla. It's amazing actually. Whatever antics a family member pulled, she just loved us all. She was never discouraging if you wanted to try something new even if she was a little worried. She would just say "Well ... if you want to try" and the decision was ultimately yours."

"I always used the word "grace" to describe my mom. The family stuck together when she was still alive. She was the magnet that pulled us to her and together. My father was an honourable man but as head of the family he was a little tougher. There was never any doubt that he loved his wife and he was always good to her."

"That's quite a love story Jane."

"Yes I guess it was. They had a hard life starting out but always had their family as their focus. I spent my mother's last few days with her. She slept most of the time. On her final day, her eyes remained open, seeming to absorb each member of the family. Her eyes remained open until her husband returned. He was able to say goodbye. She took her last breath while we were in the room with her."

"You know Myla, in order to love the best, sometimes you end up hurting the most. I made sure my mother knew how much she was loved and I was thankful for that. There is nothing I would not give to have one more day with her."

"Jane, you were blessed to have such an influence in your life. It's not always the case. I have met people that have terrible experiences with loved ones. One such person suffered abuse by her stepfather and the mother was too weak or too afraid to stand up to him and protect her children. He drank and became verbally and physically abusive and it was the children that paid for that anger."

"Myla, I can't image how some people have struggled. I was blessed but then later in life lost most of my family. It makes you wonder whether we are meant to struggle in some part of our lives in order to enjoy other parts. Makes me go back to the lessons we have come here to learn. Perhaps we need to appreciate the good times more and realize how blessed we are at the time and not later."

A Moment for You

Make sure those that are important to you know that how you feel about them and what they have added to your life. You never know when you will no longer have the chance to do so and the opportunity will have been missed.

Take the time to honour that person – write a note, use a journal or make a collage with notes about the person. Reflect on the special things. You can give your message or creation to that person so they know who they are and what they mean to you.

It's not the load that will break you,

It's the way you carry it.

Lena Horne

IT'S ALL ABOUT THE FAITH

Jane sat looking up at Myla. "I want to take you back a bit. You know we have talked about so many things but we have never touched on religion. Is that something you feel like talking about?"

Myla laughed, "Jane, you know there's not much I won't talk about."

Jane smiled and nodded knowingly. "You know, as a child, I faithfully attended church, being involved in the choir, the youth group and many other church activities. In the summer there were classes with visiting nuns and then church-related camp."

"Sometimes mass could be understood but mostly the message was lost with the muffled words quickly coming out of the mouths of the elderly priests. Then a younger priest arrived. Initially he seemed to be a good addition to the church. As time went on there were inconsistencies with his behaviour. Discrepancies between what I had been brought up to believe a priest was and some subtle things that made me question him."

Jane continued, "there were the pictures of holidays he had taken to Caribbean destinations. Always many women in each shot. I didn't' think much of it at the time. Then there was the time he put a fourteen year old girl on his lap at a dinner party. He was holding her too tight and close and she was very uncomfortable. The girl stood up and asked him to stop molesting her which shocked the other guests."

"On another occasion, a group of individuals gathered at a house and for some reason this priest had attended. Conversations with this priest consisted of his eyes focusing on the chest of any woman speaking instead of her eyes. He forced one person to sit right next to him on the couch placing his arm around her and pulling her much closer than was acceptable. It just seemed inappropriate and I remember feeling uncomfortable. I wanted to say something but we were taught that this was someone to be revered and so I didn't."

Jane sighed, "Having held previous priests in high regard, this behaviour destroyed the trust I felt in priests as well as the church. It resulted in a loss of faith that was never quite restored. The trust in religion was all but gone and it has been a long road back to connect to some form of spirituality."

Myla nodded. "When we are young we blindly follow whatever religious practice our parents followed. We naturally form our own opinions to find what feels right in our hearts. We explore what has meaning for us. It doesn't necessary mean you are rejecting your parents' values, just awakening your own awareness."

Jane added: "Priests are men. We hold them up to a standard that equates with their covenant with God. They made the choice. If they can't keep to the contracts they have made, they should remove themselves from the position of trust they are in because of those contracts. This trust is given to them because of the vows they made. It is not their right to put this trust in jeopardy."

"Yes Jane, life is full of things we can't trust and losing faith in something you have believed in for many years can be life-altering. Be careful where you place your trust and make sure it is worthy of your trust. As long as you can look in the mirror and be satisfied with the decisions you make, that's what's important."

"A little harder lesson to learn is not to let someone's mistakes ruin your own faith. It's a long road back and the longer you stay away, the harder it is to get back. Understand the difference between the religion and spirituality and see what fits for you. It is after all, your life."

A Moment for You

Is your religion one of choice or the result of someone else's choosing or guidance? Is there meaning for you in those teachings? Do you have a question in your heart about what you have been taught?

There is a huge difference between religion and spirituality. I feel you can live as a spiritual person in the way you conduct yourself every day but that doesn't necessarily find its roots in religion.

Be true to yourself. Discover what fits for you and your life. Be kind to others and be kind to yourself and live your life as a spiritual human being. Then decide for yourself what religion, if any, rings true for you.

Never underestimate the effect of clutter in your life.

Karen Kingston

HOARDING – FILLING THE EMPTINESS

When Jane hurried in to the café, she found it was a little busy. It was earlier than the usual time she dropped in. Jane's favourite table happened to be open so she wandered over pouring herself a cup of coffee on her way. It had been raining and it just mirrored the way Jane was feeling that day. She was glad she had put her hair in a ponytail or she would have looked like a drenched rat.

Myla waved as Jane walked in.

Jane smiled and just watched her.

Myla finally popped over when things slowed down a little just in time to give Jane a refresher of coffee. She gave Myla a big hug and they sat down together.

"You know Myla, we have talked about loss before. I was thinking about an after-effect of loss. I remember when my mother passed away, my father seemed to acquire a considerable amount of stuff in the house. I recall being quite concerned about this accumulation of clutter and even had some conversations with him. These conversations didn't go far and the clutter continued. My husband and I did what we could to keep the piles at bay but it was not easy. We had to remember to show respect for this was his home and not ours no matter how much it frustrated us or how concerned we were for him."

"I have heard of this from others Jane. What I have witnessed is when there is loss in someone's life, sometimes clutter seems to become a problem. I have a theory. Would you like to hear it?"

"Of course Myla. You know I would."

They laughed together.

"First Jane, clutter fills up empty space. If space is filled up it is no longer empty and perhaps makes someone feel less alone. It may even provide a sense of safety and a feeling of protection."

"Second, I have noticed that sometimes this clutter is a result of an individual continuing to bring things in that a deceased person used to enjoy and then these things just sit there."

"And thirdly, I think by being able to bring these things into a home, one might feel they are still providing for the person that is no longer there and thereby making the loss feel less intense and less painful."

"Jane, sometimes it's just hard to part with things that belonged to someone you loved."

"I am sure there are many other reasons but I do believe it is a way to compensate for a broken heart. We all suffer from broken hearts in our lives and sometimes we just need a friendly hand to help us through it. Clutter is often a result of the emptiness caused by loss in my opinion. I feel that if you look deep enough you will often find there has been a loss that someone has been unable to get over or perhaps didn't even realize it affected them but it's there and clutter becomes their way of coping."

"You know Myla, that seems to make a lot of sense and when I think of some others that have dealt with the same issue with parents or family members, the same seems to ring true."

Myla nodded. "So we need to be there to help them come to terms with the loss so they can fill their hearts with other things and learn to be happy again. To help them know they are still loved and are not alone."

"Myla, I saw this show up in one of my nieces as well. Julie never came to terms with her parent's divorce. It was still a wish that they would get back together. She really didn't want to remember how damaging the marriage had been. Afterwards, Julie held on to everything and I watched the clutter grow in her new home. Nothing was unpacked. Anything brought in just sat there. Things were mostly the way they were when she first moved in. It was so sad to see and try as I might, I felt helpless."

"Yes Jane, it's hard but you can't force anyone to get help if they don't want it."

"That was a hard pill to swallow. Julie was a big part of my life. I never dreamed we would have parted ways but we did for a while. We had shared so much. She was a beautiful, happy girl that smiled with excitement all the time. She lost that sparkle after the divorce and still struggles. I still see the sparkle in her but it will take some coaxing to get it to come back out but I would never give up on her so I keeping trying."

"Then, it actually showed up in me as well Myla. I acquired the contents of my parents' home as well as things of my brothers. That included all kinds of paperwork, photos, recipes and just memories. I found it was very hard to part with these things as well. They were all gone but their stuff was still with me. Favourite hats of my mother's. Pictures of them as a young couple. Important papers showing the history of our family."

"I held on to them wanting to pass the memories and information on to the family that remained but as time went on, I realized I was hoping that there still was a family to pass these things on to. It took time but I realized there wasn't. There was no interest in the history. There was no attachment to the memories. I was holding on to things that meant nothing to anyone but me. As I slowly let these things go, it felt like the end of the line for our family. There were others out there with the name but that's all it was in the end and for my own sake, I had to let it go."

A Moment for You

As much as you try to help someone with clutter you have to tread lightly. These people have not lost their minds. They are struggling emotionally with something and these "things" become a replacement for someone or something that is no longer there. They can't part with them because it increases their feeling of emptiness and perhaps even their helplessness over the change in their lives.

You can help but you have to involve them with the decisions and choices they have to make. Respect and patience is so important. Compassion, even when you can't understand what is happening, is crucial.

Chances are that this individual has raised you and provided for you and now they are dealing with a huge emptiness in their life. Think about how you would want to be treated and be kind.

Think of the clutter as a cry for help. If you know there is no mental illness that is the cause of the clutter, then look at it as a cry for help.

Remember, how would you like it if someone started rifling through your stuff and throwing out whatever they laid their hands on? It wouldn't make anyone very happy. Of course you have to take safety and cleanliness into account but involve them in the process and allow them to talk. They need to deal with the pain inside. Help them get it out.

Each human package

has its own unique surprise.

Jana Baron

AMAZING STRENGTH

Well today the sun was shining as Jane made her way to Soul Fire Café. She was happy to see Myla pop out from behind the swinging doors when she walked in. Smiling that big red smile, she came right over with the pot.

"Good morning Myla. How are you today?"

"Dandy, Jane, just dandy." She sat herself down and said, "what's on your mind today Janey girl? I need something to sink my teeth into. Feeling a little restless."

"Well Myla I think I can help. I was thinking about my niece the other day. Her name is Jesse. At a time when she should have been excited about entering the next phase of her life, everything changed so drastically for her."

"What happened Jane? This is a story I have not heard from you."

"You know Jesse was not feeling well and she had developed large bruises on her legs. I was taking her to get her beginner's driver's permit one day but she didn't feel well enough to go. She had been waiting for some blood test results and in the meantime, being the concerned aunt, I had researched reasons for the bruising. What I found made me somewhat anxious."

"Doesn't sound too good Jane."

"I decided not to wait for the results, picked her up and returned to the doctor's office to see if they had arrived. A different doctor examined her. The results were not in but he looked at me and told me to take Jesse directly to the Children's Hospital."

"Oh my Jane, that doesn't sound good."

"Yes Myla, it was only a few hours later that it was confirmed that she had cancer. It was devastating news."

Jane teared up but continued, "Jesse was a mixture of sensitivity and toughness. Her parents had separated a few months prior and it had been hard on her. Jesse was so brave during the course of events after the diagnosis that at times I felt she was comforting me instead of the other way around."

"She was the first niece and the first grandchild in the family. Hearts were broken for her and everyone was worried."

"Oh Jane, I can hardly imagine the pain everyone was in during that time."

"Yes. It was truly a terrible time. Once chemo started and she began to lose her hair, she decided to shave it all off. She took each step as it came so matter-of-factly and I was so amazed at her resilience. Through it all she was so strong."

"Her father did not fare so well. He was still reeling from being separated from the children he loves so much. It was a marriage that was slowly destroying him but you don't see these things when you are close up sometimes."

"He told me in later years, he should have let his wife go when she left the first time."

"Yes Jane, hindsight is always 20/20."

"Isn't that the truth Myla? Can you imagine as a teenager to be told you may never be able to be a mother?"

"My heart broke for her as I watched her fight. I felt so helpless. I loved her as if she were my own and there was nothing I could do. The treatments continued and eventually ended, her hair grew back and she gained her strength back."

"What made things worse Myla, was after that her mother decided that she wanted no influence from her husband's side of the family and pulled both children away for two years. Because of her instability and insecurity she kept everyone her children grew up around away from them. It was cruel on so many levels and only served her which is just what she wanted. She didn't want anyone's advice or help and that's how she accomplished it. I truly believe if the children had any contact with the rest of the family, she would have thrown them out."

"After a couple of years my niece slowly returned to the fold. Unfortunately, things had changed. A lot of people had been hurt. Everyone was more cautious, more guarded and less trusting. All because of one fly in the ointment."

"And how is your niece now?"

"It's amazing Myla. It's been many years. She is doing well. She was even blessed to have a child that she calls her "miracle baby"."

A MOMENT FOR YOU

Be careful who you put your trust in. Make sure they have earned it and will value it as much as you would. Many hearts and lives are broken because of lost trust. Protect your heart.

It's easy to paint people with one brush but when society says "family" is all you need, it really does depend on the family. If your family is not the kind that you can trust or if they make you doubt yourself at every instance, then your family may not be all you need and that family trust is not something you should give away blindly.

Everyone has to make their own decision about the value of their family. But if you can't trust the people you are supposed to be closest to then it's a decision only you can make for yourself.

Hanging on to resentment

is letting someone you despise

live rent-free in your head.

Ann Landers

YOU NEVER KNOW THEM AS WELL AS YOU THINK

As Jane sat spinning her spoon around in her coffee cup she looked up as Myla approached. "Time for a coffee break yet Myla?"

"Hey Jane. Just spotted you." Smiling, she looked around. "Just one sec and I'll be back."

Jane watched her bounce over to check on some customers, refilling their coffee cups and then came back relaxing into the chair.

"Let me pour that for you Myla."

As I poured a cup for Myla she thanked me. "How have you been doing Jane?"

"Myla, I still struggle to understand sometimes. It's getting easier because of our chats."

"Glad to hear it. What's on your mind today my dear?"

"You know I've never been a parent but I know I have loved as much as if I was. I have felt the pain and the pride. There is nothing I wouldn't have done for my nieces and nephews. What's still hard is that you can be so easily tossed aside like you didn't matter at all. I still don't get it."

"And you know Jane, you probably never will."

"You know I tried to support my brother's spouses. One was in my life for most of my adult years. Her children had some difficulties and they would talk to me at times about their struggles as did their mother. They were living in an unhealthy environment and it was affecting all of them. My sister-in-law stayed out of fear of being alone but so many suffered because of that choice. She would not own up to it or do anything about it. She didn't see her part in the dysfunction. One child had anger issues that even scared her. The other became apathetic and struggled with letting anything go."

"You know Myla, it's one thing to put up with bad behaviour yourself but when it starts to affect your children, that's a game changer in my opinion. I have always believed that a parent's job is to protect and guide their children otherwise why have them at all. Parents are not meant to be a child's friend."

"It was a vicious circle. They would come to me when there were problems and then go away and she would bury her head in the sand until the next time. In time it was just too difficult to see the repetitive cycle and we parted ways. I had lost my patience with the way nothing was ever addressed and she lost patience with me nattering about it. It wasn't healthy for either one of us so we went our separate ways. When I look back I see things were very different than I believed them to be."

Myla nodded and said "People have to take responsibility for their actions and if they don't, unfortunately, that is their cross to bear. It's sad, how often it affects the children in negative ways, if they allow it to."

A MOMENT FOR YOU

Be aware of those you spend your time with. If it's true what they say about being a combination of the five people you spend the most time with, then you have to choose wisely. Keep your eyes wide open. There are always signs. Nobody will look out for you as much as you should.

The most important relationship you will ever have is the one you have with yourself. That's the one you need to treat with love and respect.

What else really matters if you don't? Remember to take care of the one that is always with you.

When people go to work,

they shouldn't have to leave

their hearts at home.

B. Bender

THE PUZZLE OF WORK

As Jane watched Myla, she couldn't help but smile. What happiness she seemed to bring with that coffee. It was like a magic elixir. She made her way over for their regular chats and said her hellos to Jane.

"How are you doing Myla?"

"Well it was a really busy morning. Thank God it slowed down a little."

"Yes it seemed that way."

"So, what's on the agenda today Jane?"

"Well Myla, I was thinking, along with all the upheaval in my personal life, there was work. For so many years, my work defined me. It was almost like an extension of family for me and in the earlier days whatever was needed there took priority in my life. It made me feel like I was contributing to something bigger than myself."

"I discovered I had been passed over to work on a project because my boss didn't want to lose me so the committee was told to find someone else. I didn't get it. Why would he not have admitted that himself instead of me being told by a third party. What a different impression I would have had if the approach was direct. Instead of feeling valued, I felt undermined."

"Another employer asked me to come in while recovering from surgery. My employer advised he would have to let one of the two employees go. This manoeuvre should have been written up in the journal of "What not to do as an Employer!" He didn't even tell us which one it would be so "Happy Recovery"."

"Another place of employment saw my boss replaced by a person of questionable character. I felt I would be unable to trust this individual and suggested to him that I move to another department. The new boss indicated that I should stay and for a short time I did. Things happened and it was obvious that this man would say whatever he felt someone needed to hear. I quit and after I left, I was told that this particular man said he didn't think it would work out anyway. Why not be honest about this during the initial conversation. I had offered him an out. No hard feelings, let's move on with our lives. I will never understand why people can't just be honest. Honesty doesn't have to equate with hurtful."

"Later along my career path I found a boss that I trusted and enjoyed working with. Work was still work but it felt like a good work pairing. Time went by and another employee was transferred from a department where she was experiencing difficulties. This new person velcroed herself to the boss and then took over an area of work that I was training to do. The situation disintegrated quite quickly after that resulting in the boss no longer working at the office. Unfortunately, leading up to this event were months of lost time, lies and deceit. Honesty and awareness would have made the entire situation disappear but that often seems to be the last choice made."

Myla sat and listened thoughtfully. "It's been my experience that more often than not, people are out for their place in the workplace. They are there to help their own growth and serve their own reason for being there. It's probably not the best idea to be so loyal to someone else that you lose focus on what's best for you."

"So true Myla," Jane added. "And I am sure I did that for a long while. Some lessons are harder to learn than others!"

A Moment for You

Remember a job is just that – a job. Keep your integrity intact, do the best job you can and remember your life is separate and needs at least as much attention and time as you give your job.

Do you come home feeling satisfied with your job at the end of the day or are you exhausted from the work or perhaps the drama? If you can figure out what is causing you to feel that way, then you are well on your way to making it different. Finding out the why is where you need to start? Is it overwork, overwhelm, drama, disrespect, boredom or something else? Figure out why and then you can figure out how to deal with it.

Pay attention to your gut instinct. If it feels like a fish, looks like a fish and smells like a fish, chances are it's not a potato! We cause ourselves more grief by analyzing and dissecting what a situation may or may not be. Trust yourself to know what's best for you.

Don't be afraid to stand up for yourself and never live in fear of your job. If you are fearful of losing your job or being demoted, you are giving your power to someone else which only serves to increase your level of fear or becomes a self-fulfilling prophecy.

You are who you are and deserve to find work where you flourish and are appreciated. Now, I am not saying leave your job if it is not a financially sound or viable option, but if you need to move on, start looking at what you really want, what you need to do to get there and then start moving. You are the only one responsible for your life. I gave my power away for far too long and unfortunately the only people that served were the ones I gave my power away to. Don't get lost in what's best for someone else.

"The most important thing is this:

to sacrifice what you are now

for what you can become tomorrow."
— <u>Shannon L. Alder</u>

THE POWER OF RELEASE

As Jane sat in her usual spot she says, "You know Myla, I have learned so much about looking at life differently from you. You have helped me in so many ways and yet I have never asked how did you become so wise about life and yet always seem so happy?"

Myla smiled her usual warm smile and sighed. "It wasn't always this way. I have had my struggles and fought my battles. I have held my grudges. I have learned that it is true that holding grudges is like drinking poison and hoping the other person dies. It was silly and made no sense. It didn't make me feel better. In fact it made me feel worse. I came to believe that after a hurtful event, I would be a distant memory to the other person. It was only me holding on to the grudge and that only hurt me. So, I had to learn to let go and let it be. I believed that these people came in to my life to teach me something and I began to think in a new way. I also went a step further and thought if they were here to teach me something, who says they weren't here to learn their own lessons and if that is the case, who am I to stand in the path of their lessons."

"I stopped being hurt. I stopped being angry. I forgave. Not for them but I forgave for me. I made peace with the one in the mirror. From that moment I chose to live a life without regret."

"Jane, people generally come to the coffee shop to unwind, regroup or just rest a bit. The world is always racing and this is where they stop and say "WHOA". Well, she laughs, they don't really say that but that's what I see! Instead of being filled with bitterness and resentment, I decided to make it my mission in life to bring a smile with the coffee. It may be the only smile they see that day. If my simple smile helps their heart warm a little then it was worth it. The reactions aren't always pleasant but again, that reaction to my smile is from their perspective and I can't change that. I can just keep trying and hope it helps others along the way."

Jane sat there nodding knowingly. "Your smile, your big heart and all you have taught me has definitely helped me. I want to thank you for opening my eyes and changing my view. I will live a life without regret from this moment forward. I was blessed to walk through your door at a time I needed to open my eyes. I thank you from the bottom of my heart. Never ever stop smiling Myla."

THE PASSING OF THE TORCH

Jane was on her way back to Soul Fire Café. This time was different. It had been a while and this time she was bringing a friend. Myla had been there to help her in working through so many of her difficulties and she was ever so grateful. She knew Myla would be able to assist her friend as well.

Jane opened the door and looked around. She couldn't see her favourite coffee lady. They sat down and a young lady came over to serve them. Jane asked "Where's Myla?"

"Oh, she left last week. Seems an old flame from her past met her here quite by accident and after a few weeks, they decided to move on together. She seemed to be very happy and he seemed to really care about her."

Jane smiled and said "No one deserves it more. I will miss her and our many conversations. I was hoping to have her talk to my friend."

The waitress tilted her head and said "You don't happen to be Jane, do you?

"I sure am."

"Well hold on one second. Myla left something for you. Let me see if I can find it."

She quickly returned with an envelope and a beautiful box.

Jane stared for a moment wondering what this woman, a stranger who, while pouring coffee, became such a dear friend, could have left for her.

She slowly opened the box. Inside she found a beautiful crystal heart. It had bevelled edges and reflected light in all different colours. She understood immediately and her eyes filled with tears.

She then slowly opened the envelope and found a letter.

"My Dearest Jane:

I had hoped to see you one more time before I left but it was not to be. I had no way to find you as our only connection was the time we spent together at Soul Fire Café.

I have set out on a new adventure which my heart feels is the right choice. I hope you have returned and this letter has found its way to you.

I wanted you to know I will miss our conversations. I know you have struggled but you have also grown so much during our time together. I wish only good things for you and for your future, bearing in mind that the difficult things are what makes us learn and grow. How can you enjoy a beautiful sunrise without the darkness of the night?

I hope you will treasure this heart as a symbol of our sharing. It represents so many things. The angles signify life and are different for everyone. No two people have the same trials or are affected the same way because our histories are never the same. But it is those histories that make us who we are. It's the false beliefs that we hold that may keep us down but the strength comes from our histories.

The lights and colours that glow in different directions are symbols of the gifts we carry within us to help ourselves and others overcome obstacles so all of our hearts will sparkle again.

And lastly, the heart is precious and we need to look after it for ourselves and what we run into on our journey.

Please accept this heart as my gift to you. Think of it often as you move through your life. We have gathered much information from our time together. Use what you have learned and think what a wonderful world it could be if we stopped being angry and hating for no reason. Never forget that the only person you can truly change is yourself.

Do your best, be your best and watch things change, even if it's only for one person. Be the start of your own ripple. I sense it will be a large one. Hold the heart as a reminder to hold other hearts until they are healed like yours.

I will never forget you Jane.

Love, Myla"

With tears streaming down her face, Jane folder up the letter, stared a little longer at the box and then closed it.

Her friend, not knowing what was going on, just stared at Jane.

Jane took a deep breath and looked at her friend.

I am so sorry you were unable to meet Myla. I am sure you would have loved her as I did.

With a deep sigh, she continued. I know we came here for a reason. I am willing to listen if you are willing to talk. Perhaps together we can find some answers." And thus began Jane's next journey.

EPILOGUE

When I started writing this book, it was from a place of darkness. Perhaps I was trying to ease my pain or help others along the way. Maybe I didn't know my reason. What happened as a result was I reconnected to myself. I always said I no longer knew who I was after the losses. But ... what if I was wrong? What if putting everybody's needs before mine is where I disconnected from myself? Once the losses happened, the family was gone, I realized I had been forgotten for a long time. I had stopped doing the things I loved so many years ago.

Things changed when I married. We did things for everyone else because that was who we were. We put ourselves last. We bought a house that could house my parents if and when the time came. Instead it housed my brothers.

I closed a business to be there for my ailing mother. Some decisions I wouldn't change. Many others I would. We got lost in being part of the family and as a result, lost sight of who we were.

I have added a few stories about some of the people I was fortunate enough to get to know and help. They are people I was happy and proud to know.

I used to feel that you had to have endured great pain before you had a story to tell. I no longer believe that. We have all suffered and felt our own pain and we all have a story worth telling. Your story doesn't have to be in written form. It can just be a story you share with someone. Even if it is only one person that can understand your story, if you can help that one person, isn't that enough?

So, tell your story. Someone is waiting. And in the telling, you get to remember "Who Am I Now?" and in the end it really is worth it.

THE NEXT GENERATION OF SOUL CONNECTIONS

RITA

Rita was referred to me from a coach in another country. She was so very sad. Her health made her unable to work. She had lost her mother and her sister in a very short time. She moved to be closer to her sister's child but she couldn't help but feel in limbo immersed in the losses she had experienced.

My heart went out to her. She felt so alone and wanted to give up but I sensed something in her voice that told me she just needed to find a way through the sadness. She had nowhere to put the hurt, the guilt and the overwhelming sadness she felt. I knew that to feel such pain, she had to have such capacity for love in her heart. I knew she just had to find that love for herself.

Since we lived in different countries, we worked together over the phone. As we worked together, through the tears, some laughter started to come through. Her heart slowly started to open up again and allowed some of the pain out.

We went through a process called grief recovery and she was able to let go of things she no longer needed to hold on to. The guilt no longer served her so she let it go. Although she would always miss her family, the stabbing ache that was there whenever she thought of them dissipated. She finished the conversations she was unable to have because of the deaths and her heart became more peaceful. She came through what she referred to as "the darkest night of her soul" to wanting to live again.

Rita is a gift to this world and she started to see what work she may have to venture into. She was starting to think about possibilities for her future. Rita was kind, compassionate and could teach others to find their way. I applauded her courage and her huge heart.

I was truly happy to be able to help her navigate this journey and find some peace.

DAVIS

Davis came to me feeling he had been unable to get over the death of his wife several years prior. I felt really unsure if I would be able to help him. He was a Minister and a spiritual man. I wondered what I would be able to offer someone who would be skilled at helping others heal.

I believe in what I do so we agreed to proceed together. As we went through some steps some interesting discoveries started to surface. He and his wife had met and fueled each other's addictive behaviours. Eventually some of the addictions were conquered and his wife was instrumental in reconnecting Davis and his father.

His wife subsequently became very ill and Davis witnessed some terrible moments through the illness up to her death. Illness can be just as horrific for the caregiver as it is for the patient, maybe even worse, because they feel so helpless.

As we continued the process, Davis came to realize it was actually the relationship with his father that he had never come to terms with. His wife was the conduit that had brought them back together.

Bravely pushing through the pain and the tears, Davis was able to heal the part of him that he carried since he was a teenager. He had been dishonest with his father and realized he had never forgiven himself. As a result he had abused himself with alcohol and drugs most of his life.

I am sure his father would have or even may have forgiven him years ago but Davis held it in, unknowingly, until we discovered it together. Davis was a good man but felt less than for a long time in his life. It kept him stuck in an unhealthy lifestyle for many years. It was time to say goodbye to the pain and find a way to forgive himself and that is what he did.

I connected with Davis a few months later. He told me he had quit smoking and drinking. He was happier than he had been in a long time. He said "You saved my life" and I couldn't have been happier for him.

The tools are so simple but so effective for people to uncover and then move past pain that holds them back. Being open to discovering what might be in your way and letting it go can heal your heart and allow you to become whole again.

The beliefs held by Davis made him make choices that were dangerous because he wanted to bury the pain. After our work, he was at peace and happy.

It was some months later I heard Davis had passed. I was blessed to have played a small part in his transformation and hope he passed with peace in his heart. He certainly deserved that.

KERRY

I met this woman once and we became friends right away. My heart broke for her as she was so sad and in such emotional pain.

Her husband of many years left her for another without warning. He had deceitfully driven her to sign off papers letting go of her ownership in his company before he told her he was leaving her. She did so because she loved him and would have done anything he asked. She trusted him and believed what she was doing would help him in some way.

Instead of honouring that, he used it to defraud her. They had been married for years and she couldn't even begin to comprehend why he would do this to her. All she ever did was love him.

She was devastated. She lost all belief in herself and felt she had done something wrong. It took many conversations and many tears. Over time the tears slowed. Kerry grew stronger and started to believe in herself once again.

This beautiful woman went from being on top of the world, a beautiful home, anything she wanted and having what she thought was a happy marriage to nothing. She was in complete shock. She had to find a job with only the skills she had as a homemaker. It was hard but she grew stronger. She was bright and funny and although she was hurting, her love of life began to shine through. She was so determined. She began to see her husband for what he was. She recognized that she was not the deceitful one and that this was not her doing. She became a priority in her own life and her confidence soared.

When we lose ourselves in a marriage or relationship it is easy to miss the signs but they are usually there. We often choose to ignore them. The signing off of the papers was a huge flag but she did it for the right reasons. He was, after all, her husband of many years. He wouldn't hurt her.

Losing yourself gives away your power. On the one hand you should always have a priority position in your own life. On the other hand, giving anyone that much power over you is a lot of responsibility to place in the hands of another. We have to always be responsible for our own lives and for our own happiness. No one can provide that for you.

As time went on, Kerry educated herself and became certified in her field of interest in her sixties. She is one amazing lady. She bought a new home and lives her life happily. She takes care of herself and is as beautiful on the inside as she is on the outside. I am lucky and blessed to know her.

A quote from Kerry – "There is no later. You have to do it now!"

ABOUT THE AUTHOR

Lesia Zablockij created Soul Fire Café as a place to heal barriers to happiness. She wanted Soul Fire Cafe to be that place for others because she couldn't find it when she needed it.

Lesia helps people find some of those missing pieces of their life's puzzle. The life she once knew disintegrated before her very eyes and she had to uncover those missing pieces to move into the next part of her life. Lesia searched for the answer to the question "**Who am I Now?**" because everything she knew about her life no longer existed.

As Lesia studied, she discovered that people have long-held beliefs and those beliefs are a major factor for self-sabotage. These beliefs are the reason that people are not where they thought they would be or where they want to be in life. Lesia examines those beliefs by uncovering old defining moments and then helping her clients create new ones.

In order to make changes, you have to start with self-awareness and that is the groundwork of Soul Fire Café. From self-awareness to healing barriers to happiness to igniting your soul.

Lesia found many assessments were a great tool for self-discovery. She acquired several designations to enable her to administer a variety of assessments and related programs. Lesia works one-on-one and with groups offering one day or up to 12 week workshops in person or by teleseminar. Some of the designations and certifications she holds are:

- **Associate Certified Coach with the International Coach Federation**

- **Core Temperament Essentials Trainer and Coach**

- **Now What? Authorized Facilitator (90 days to a new Life Direction)**

- **Grief Recovery Specialist**

- **Robbins Madanes Strategic Intervention Coach (in progress)**

- **Sacred Money Archetype Coach**

- **Coach U Core Essentials Graduate**

- **Certified Print Coach**

- *Myers Briggs Facilitator*

- *Certified Story Coach*

- *Life Purpose Institute Life and Career Coach*

- *Strategic Learning Alliance Certified Professional Coach*

- *Jack Canfield Success Principles Coach Graduate*

- *Barbara Sher Success Team Leader*

- *Career/Employment Counselor (Honors)*

Lesia invites you to enter Soul Fire Café. She would love to hear your story. It has been a long journey for Lesia to get here. She would be honoured to help you shorten your journey and heal your barriers to happiness.

Made in the USA
Charleston, SC
28 March 2015